Paula Lyons

I DREAM THINGS
THAT NEVER WERE...
AND SAY WHY NOT

Best wishes
for a happy holiday
happy

M. C.

Quotations of
ROBERT F. KENNEDY

I DREAM THINGS
THAT NEVER WERE...

AND SAY WHY NOT

Selected by
Jane Wilkie
and Rod McKuen

STANYAN BOOKS

RANDOM HOUSE

A Stanyan book
Published by Stanyan Books,
8721 Sunset Blvd., Suite C
Los Angeles, California 90069,
and by Random House, Inc.
201 E. 50th Street,
New York, N.Y. 10022

Designed by Hy Fujita

Printed in U.S.A.

PREFACE

What kind of a man was Robert F. Kennedy?

According to those who knew him, he was impetuous, given to speaking in a sort of shorthand his listeners found difficult to follow, yet fond of a precise phrase. He once ignored the apology of an airline stewardess who had stumbled over his feet in the aisle, yet he also stood silently for twenty minutes, holding the hand of a dying stranger in a home for the aged. He took pride in the fact he had many enemies, yet he was loved by thousands. He was shy, yet often described as ruthless—an adjective that seemed to amuse him.

He was a complex man, seemingly without the heroics of his brother Joe, the grace of his brother John, or the handsomeness of his brother Ted. He stayed in the background, investigating for the Rackets Committee and working tirelessly for the advancement of John F. Kennedy.

Five years after the assassination of President Kennedy, the public Robert Kennedy was just beginning to emerge; he began to assert himself, to be beloved by young America, when he was shot down in the kitchen of a Los Angeles hotel, on June 4, 1968.

A man's words are the brush of his self-portrait; here are things Robert F. Kennedy said, in public and private, which help to paint the man.

Jane Wilkie

INTRODUCTION

I DREAM THINGS THAT NEVER WERE AND SAY
WHY NOT

INTRODUCTION

Robert Kennedy was not a guru, nor the leader of
a cult, nor a big-brother figure, nor a hero destined
to lead us into new battles. He was instead perhaps the personification of what the common man
needs and wants from a leader. To the youth of
this country he was a friend, and to all of us a
coming alternative to the kind of politics and bu-
reaucracy that has become the daily smog of our
lives. He was a friend of mine and a friend of
many. What he said and did during his short life
will remain important in the world, throughout
our lifetime and beyond.

Rod McKuen

'Some men see things as they are
and say why. I dream things
that never were and say why not.'

Whenever men take the law into
their own hands, the loser is
the law. And when the law
loses, freedom languishes.
                    1961

If any man claims the Negro
should be content... let him say
he would willingly change the color
of his skin and go to live in the
Negro section of a large city.
Then and only then has he a
right to such a claim.

1966

There are two major ways to communicate
what this country is really about: to
bring people here, or to send
Americans abroad.

1966

Right now, as a senator, I'm
dealing only with my own personal
future. It's not so important, . . .
not as important as it was, as it
used to be.

1967

We were all involved in certain
tasks, in certain dreams.

1967

Freedom and justice—for me
these are the meaning of America.
                1965

Most of our fellow citizens do their
best—and do it the modest, un-
spectacular, decent, natural way,
which is the highest form of public service.
But every day in a shameful variety of ways, the
selfish actions of the small
minority sully the honor of our nation.
                1961

I'd like to harness all the energy
and effort and incentive and
imagination that was attracted
to government by President Kennedy.
I don't want any of that to die ...
If I could figure out some course
for me that would keep all that
alive and utilize it for the
country, that's what I'd do.
                    1964

I don't think it (the American Nazi
party) is a threat. I think they're
a little like those people in the
United States during that nostalgic
period thirty years ago, who used to go
around swallowing goldfish. I think
we will always have people who are a
little odd. And if you join the Nazi
party now, you're very odd.
                    1966

Every year the average New Yorker
... breathes in 750 pounds of his
own wastes ... Because there are
so many of us ... we must breathe
the same air into which we care-
lessly spill our refuse.
                    1967

Crime is ... a reproach to the
moral pretensions of our society,
and advertises to the world the
gap between our pronouncements
and our performance.
                    1962

Our legacy ... will be the role and
standing of the United States in the
world—whether, in short, people will
look to this country with hope or with
hate, emulation or envy.
                    1966

This country has been built on
the foundation that the government doesn't do everything; that
the neighbor helps his
neighbor.

1962

I think there is an obligation on the
part of all of us to stay informed
and aware.

1966

We are all Americans. To attack the
motives of those who express
concern about our present course—
to challenge their very right to
speak freely—is to strike at the
foundation of the democratic
process which our fellow citizens . . .
are dying in order to protect.

1966

There is freedom in this country to be
extreme, to propose the most re-
actionary or the most utopian
solutions to . . . problems. There is
freedom here to believe and act
with passion, whether for the cause
of religion or party or personal
welfare.

1964

New answers must be found by us.
They must be worked out not only in
the quiet contemplation of the study,
but in the dust and sweat, the swirl
and thunder of the arena. And they
must be, above all, dispassionate—
determined not by the prejudices we
bring to a problem, but by the facts
we find in it.

1966

We are a great country, an unselfish
country and a compassionate country.

June 4, 1968

It is the essence of responsibility
to put the public good ahead of
personal gain.
                    1964

Ours is a time when many things
are just too big to be grasped.
                    1961

The strength of the free press
of this country goes beyond
epigrams. The press is the
base on which democracy rests
in a complex twentieth-century
society.
                    1965

We have a responsibility to the
victims of crime and violence.
It is a responsibility . . . to make
the possession and use of firearms
a matter undertaken only by
serious people who will use them
with the restraint and maturity
that their dangerous nature deserves . . .
It is past time that we wipe this stain
of violence from our land.

(89th Congress)

There is a tremendous advantage
in having the same last name as
the President of the United States.
1962

I'm not running a popularity contest.
It doesn't matter if people like me
or not. Jack can be nice to them.
I don't try to antagonize people, but
somebody has to be able to say no.
If people are not getting off their
behinds, how do you say that nicely?
1960

A lot of people think I'm out of
my mind. You could almost get
a unanimous opinion on that.
1967

We develop the kind of citizens
we deserve.
                    1964

Laws are administered to protect
and expand individual freedom,
not to compel individuals to
follow the logic other men
impose on them.
                    1962

We have the capacity to destroy the
world even after being attacked;
but . . . will we have the capacity
for patience and restraint to
save the world after being provoked?
                    1966

I have no Presidential aspirations—
nor does my wife, Ethel Bird.
                    1964

It isn't that I'm a saint. It's
just that I've never found it necessary to be a sinner.

The cost of campaigning has become so
high that to make a candidate and
his views well known in a state like
California or New York is impossible
without either a well-known personality
or enormous sums of money. *(Pause)*
As an unknown virtually without
funds, I was, of course, an exception.
                    1967

My views on birth control are some-
what distorted by the fact I was
seventh of nine children.
1964

I received a prize of being the
fellow with the fifth best sense
of humor in my graduating class.
1962

When Mr. Khrushchev reported that the
Cosmonauts…reported seeing "no
signs of God," we can only suggest
that they aim—with the rest of
mankind—a little higher.
1963

I have no sympathy with those who are
defeatists and who would rather be
"Red than dead." Nor do I have
sympathy with those who, in the name of
fighting Communism, sow seeds of sus-
picion and distrust by making false
or irresponsible charges...against
the foundations of our government: Congress,
the Supreme Court, and even the Presidency
itself.

1964

As Attorney General, in speech to
Justice Department employees…

I came to this department ten years
ago as an assistant attorney making
$4200 a year. But I had ability and
integrity, an interest in my work.
I stayed late hours, my brother became
President, and now I'm Attorney General.
(Pause). Those qualifications were not
necessarily listed in their order of
importance.

1961

I for one would not be happy to see
this nation bland and homogeneous,
its speech and literature reduced
to the common denominator...What
would *Abie's Irish Rose* have been
if Abie was Jewish and Rose Irish
in *name* only?
                    1967

I happen to believe that the 1954
decision [on school segregation] was
right, but my belief does not matter—
it is the law. Some of you may believe
the decision was wrong. That does not matter.
It is the law.
                    1961

We are dedicated to the propo-
sition that liberty and law
are inseparable.
1962

The riots which have taken place
are an intolerable threat to the
most essential interests of every
American—black or white—to
the mind's peace and the body's
safety and the community's order,
to all that makes life worthwhile.
1966

The challenge of politics and public
service is to discover what is
interfering with justice and
dignity for the individual…and then
to decide swiftly upon the appropriate
remedies.
                1964

The business of parties is not just to
win elections. It is to govern. And
a party cannot govern if it is disunited.
1965

Ultimately, Communism must be defeated
by progressive political programs which
wipe out the poverty,
misery and discontent on which it
thrives.
1964

The Alliance for Progress was not
meant to be a means for the U.S. to
determine the governments of every
American nation.
1966

Those of us who are white can only
dimly guess at what the pain of
racial discrimination must be...
How can a Negro father explain this
intolerable situation to his
children? And how can the children
be expected to grow up with any
sense of pride in being Americans?
1963

Old age is something that happens
to everybody, and if we are wise
enough and unselfish enough and
effective enough, then we can
make those years a time in which
to live, not just linger.
1966

Government belongs wherever evil
needs an adversary and there
are people in distress who
cannot help themselves.
1964

I'd die if I made a girl cry. I
don't think I've ever made my wife
cry.
                    1966

A source of anguish...under the law, an
American citizen born in one country can
get a maid or a gardener overnight from
another country, but must wait a year or
more to be reunited with his mother.
                    1965

Here in America today, perhaps the
clearest mirror of our performance,
the truest measure of whether we
live up to our ideals, is our
youth.
                    1967

I believe that as long as most men
are honest, corruption is twice
vicious.

1964

The intolerant man will not rely on
persuasion, or on the worth of an
idea. He would deny to others the
very freedom of opinion or of
dissent which he so stridently
demands for himself. He cannot
trust democracy.

1964

Welfare workers, or higher
welfare payments, cannot confer
self-respect or self-confidence
in men without work—for in
the United States, you are
what you do.

1966

We are finding that the most
important thing is to help men to help
themselves. This is the most difficult
task of all.

1965

The real point about sacrifice,
except in times of open warfare, is
surely that it tends to be un-
dramatic, prolonged, and irritating.

1966

I believe that as long as a single
man may try, any unjustifiable
barrier against his efforts is
a barrier against mankind.

1964

There are those, frustrated by a
difficult future, who grab out for
the security of a nonexistent past...
they search for the haven of
doctrine.

1964

Moral courage is a rarer commodity than bravery in battle or great intelligence. Yet it is the one essential, vital quality for those who seek to change a world which yields most painfully to change.

1966

History is a relentless master. It has no present, only the past rushing into the future. To try to hold fast is to be swept aside.

1966

Who knows whether any of us will still be alive in 1972? Existence is so fickle, fate is so fickle.

1967

The need to halt the spread of
nuclear weapons must be a central
priority of American policy.
                    1965

We have a responsibility—to the
rest of the world and to our own
children—to find a solution to
the Vietnam problem.
                    1966

We are stronger, and therefore have
more responsibility, than any
nation on earth...we should make
the first...greatest...and last
effort to control nuclear weapons.
We can and must begin immediately.
                    1965

Governments must be strong wherever
madness threatens the peace.
                1964

If we are to leave our children
on a planet on which to live
safely, to fulfill the bright
promise of their lives, we must
resume the journey toward peace.
                1966

The young are going ahead in
their own way and in their own
time…Across the globe they
are a force of whirlwind
proportions, and the world of tomorrow

will bear the imprint of
their ideals and their goals.
For this reason, we must be concerned about
them.

1964

I believe that in this generation
those with the courage to enter
the moral conflict will find themselves with companions in every
corner of the world.
1966

If our times are difficult and per-
plexing, so are they challenging
and filled with opportunity.
1961

The right to criticize carries with it
a responsibility—to study the facts,
to be fully informed...But they [our
young people] must also be willing to
listen while others speak; and they
must be willing to have their views
tested in the marketplace of ideas.
1965

A revolution is coming—a revolution
which will be peaceful if we are wise
enough; compassionate if we care
enough; successful if we are fortunate
enough—but a revolution which is
coming whether we will it or not.
We can affect its character; we cannot
alter its inevitability.
　　　　　1966

Those who are serious about the
future have the obligation to
direct those energies and talents
toward concrete objectives con-
sistent with the ideals they
profess.
　　　　　1966

On this generation of Americans falls
the full burden of proving to the
world that we really mean it when we
say all men are created free and are
equal before the law.
　　　　　1961

The future...will belong to
those who can see that wisdom can
only emerge from the clash of
contending views, the passionate
expression of deep and hostile
beliefs.

1966

I think that some of the demon-
strations have weakened the
position of those who advocate a
particular cause. But this
doesn't mean they are illegal.

1966

The future does not belong to those
who are content with today...timid
and fearful in the face of new ideas
and bold projects.
1966

Every generation inherits a world
it never made; and as it does so,
it automatically becomes the
trustee of that world for those
who come after.
1963

To say that the future will be different from the present and past can be denounced as radicalism or branded as subversion...It hardly seems necessary to point out in the United States, of all places, that change, although it involves risks, is the law of life.

1964

We cannot solve delinquency by building new prisons. We must create new opportunities for our nation's youth.

1962

I think we can end the divisions in the United States. What I think is quite clear is that we can work together in the last analysis.

June 4, 1968

Sixty percent of the seafood taken from
water surrounding the United
States is dependent on coastal
bays and marshes for their
existence. If we destroy
these wetlands...we will also
destroy our fisheries...A shore
line with no fish, wildlife or
natural marshland would be
desolate. For these animals and
fields of marsh grass are as
much a part of our heritage as
our mountains and great rivers.
1966

Nothing is more urgent than the obligation to disenthrall ourselves from
the dogmas of the quiet past.
1964